PASSOVER

by Gloria Koster

PEBBLE
a capstone imprint

Published by Pebble, an imprint of Capstone
1710 Roe Crest Drive, North Mankato, Minnesota 56003
capstonepub.com

Library of Congress Cataloging-in-Publication Data is available on the Library of Congress website.

ISBN: 9780756576929 (hardcover)
ISBN: 9780756577100 (paperback)
ISBN: 9780756577117 (ebook PDF)

Summary: Passover is a Jewish holiday that celebrates the story of the Israelites escaping from Egypt and returning home. People take extra care in preparing their homes. They also gather with family and friends for a big meal and activities that represent the story. Discover how people around the world celebrate this holiday.

Editorial Credits
Editor: Ericka Smith; Designer: Kayla Rossow; Media Researcher: Svetlana Zhurkin; Production Specialist: Katy LaVigne

Image Credits
Alamy: Chronicle, 6, Lebrecht Music & Arts, 5, 9, Spencer Grant, 20; Dreamstime: Vetre Antanaviciute-meskauskiene, cover; Getty Images: halbergman, 26, Michael Loccisano, 16, patrickheagney, 15, pushlama, 1, Star Tribune/Jerry Holt, 19, Uriel Sinai, 11; Newscom: Zuma Press/TASS/ Mikhail Tereshchenko, 17; Shutterstock: David Cohen 156, 13, dnaveh, 21, gal mashiach, 18, Inna Reznik, 27, 29, jefftakespics2, 24, Rafal Kulik (background), back cover and throughout, rontav, 25, vetre, 23

All internet sites appearing in back matter were available and accurate when this book was sent to press.

Printed and bound in China. 5593

TABLE OF CONTENTS

Words in **bold** are in the glossary.

THE STORY OF PASSOVER

Passover is a Jewish holiday. It celebrates a story from the Hebrew Bible.

In the Hebrew Bible, Jews were called **Israelites**. They lived in Canaan. A **famine** forced them to leave. They went to Egypt.

At first, life in Egypt was good. But the ruler of Egypt—**Pharaoh**—turned against them. He enslaved the Israelites. They were forced to work. They built cities and roads.

Israelites enslaved in Egypt

Marking Jewish homes

Moses was the Israelites' leader. He asked Pharaoh to let them go. Pharaoh refused.

God was angry. He punished the Egyptians with ten **plagues**. People got sick. Crops failed. Food spoiled.

The last plague was the worst. The Angel of Death visited Egyptian families. It took away their oldest sons.

But Jewish homes had a mark. The Angel of Death saw the mark and passed over their homes. That is how the holiday got its name.

Pharaoh was afraid. He freed the Israelites. Then he changed his mind. He sent his army after them.

God helped the Israelites escape. He made a path so that they could walk across the sea. Pharaoh's army could not catch them.

The Israelites were free. They began their journey home through the desert. It took 40 years.

Passover celebrates the Israelites' freedom and their return home.

The Israelites crossing the sea

WHEN IS PASSOVER?

The Jewish calendar follows the cycles of the moon and the sun. Holidays take place during certain seasons. The dates for Passover change each year. It takes place during the Hebrew month of Nisan. Some years it is in March. Some years it is in April.

Passover usually lasts for eight days. In Israel it lasts for seven days. Like all other Jewish holidays, it begins at sundown.

People gathering together to pray during Passover in Jerusalem, Israel

HOW IS PASSOVER CELEBRATED?

GETTING READY

Before Passover, people clean house. They scrub their kitchens. They also get rid of cake, bread, cereal, and pasta. These foods are called **chametz**. During Passover, people don't eat **leavened** grains like wheat, oat, and barley. They eat matzah—a flat bread—instead.

Rolling out matzah dough

Matzah represents part of the Passover story. Israelites left Egypt quickly. They lived in the desert and were always on the move. Bread had no time to rise. So they ate matzah.

FOLLOWING THE RULES

Passover has strict rules. For the first day or two of Passover, some people don't work. At the end of Passover, some people take another day or two off from work.

In addition to chametz, some other foods are not allowed. For example, Ashkenazi Jews do not eat rice, corn, beans, or peas during the holiday.

Some families use separate cooking pots for Passover. Some homes even have a Passover kitchen. It's used only on this holiday!

BEGINNING AND ENDING PASSOVER

On the first night of Passover, families gather for a special dinner. It is called a **Seder**. Some families have one Seder. Others have a Seder two nights in a row.

Some Jewish people observe the end of Passover too. On the last two days, they may pray at home or at **synagogue**.

PASSOVER TRADITIONS

During Passover grown-ups drink wine. Children drink grape juice. There is also a cup for Elijah. He was a wise man. Some people set an extra place for him at the table. They open their doors to welcome him. But Elijah is invisible, so children love to watch his cup. Does the wine disappear?

A cup set out for Elijah

A Miriam's Cup

Some families also have a Miriam's Cup. It honors women and girls. In the Passover story, God gave Miriam a magical well so that Israelites could drink in the desert. Miriam's Cup is filled with water.

THE SEDER

The Seder is a big meal. It is also a service. There is a specific setting for the table, and the service follows a set order.

THE PASSOVER TABLE

The Passover table has certain items. There are three pieces of matzah. A cloth covers each one separately. And every table has a Seder plate.

Each Seder plate holds five or six foods. They represent the Israelites' struggles:

1. A roasted lamb shank bone

2. A roasted egg

3. A spring vegetable like parsley, which will be dipped in salt water that represents tears

4. **Charoset**—a mix of fruit, nuts, and wine—that represents the mortar the Israelites used to build with bricks when they were enslaved

5. Horseradish, which reminds Jewish people of bitter times

6. Another bitter herb or vegetable

A Seder plate

DIFFERENT KINDS OF FOOD

Jewish families have **ancestors** from different places, so the food they eat is different. Ashkenazi Jews come from Northern and Central Europe. Their Seder meal may include fish dumplings called gefilte fish. There is usually matzah ball soup. **Brisket** or roast chicken are main dishes. And there may be chocolate cake—without flour.

gefilte fish

Sephardic Jews come from Spain and Portugal. Mizrahi Jews come from the Middle East and Africa. Their meals are light and colorful. Meats and fish are prepared with vegetables and spices. Fruits like dates and apricots may be added.

THE SERVICE

The Seder begins with lighting candles and blessing the wine. Then everyone washes their hands.

Next, they bless the spring vegetable. They dip it in salt water and eat it.

A family washing their hands during a Seder

Next, a grown-up breaks the middle piece of matzah. They hide the larger piece—the **afikomen**.

Then, the youngest child asks four questions. The answers tell the Passover story. A leader reads from a special book called the *Haggadah*.

Everyone washes their hands again. The leader blesses the matzah. Guests eat pieces of plain matzah. Then they eat pieces with bitter herbs and with charoset. Finally, it's time for dinner!

After the meal, children look for the afikomen. The winner gets a prize. Then, the afikomen becomes part of the dessert.

The door is opened for Elijah.

The service ends with a final blessing. But the guests continue with stories and songs. They praise God for their freedom.

GLOSSARY

afikomen (ah-fee-KOH-mehn)—the larger piece of a broken piece of matzah that's hidden during a Seder

ancestor (AN-ses-tuhr)—a family member who lived a long time ago

brisket (BRIS-kit)—a cut of beef

chametz (kah-MAYTZ)—grains that have been allowed to rise

charoset (kah-ROH-set)—a mixture of fruit, nuts, and wine

famine (FA-muhn)—a serious shortage of food resulting in widespread hunger and death

Israelite (IZ-ree-uh-lite)—the name for a Jewish person in the Bible

leavened (LEV-uhnd)—something that has risen

Pharaoh (FEY-roh)—the leader of Egypt in the Bible

plague (PLAYG)—a widespread problem, like a disease

Seder (SAY-duhr)—a meal that takes place during Passover

synagogue (SIN-a-gog)—a building where Jewish people come together to pray

READ MORE

Basseri, Etan. *A Persian Passover*. Moosic, PA: Kalaniot Books, 2022.

Hamen, Susan E. *Passover*. Minneapolis: DiscoverRoo, 2021.

Koster, Gloria. *Rosh Hashanah*. North Mankato, MN: Capstone, 2024.

INTERNET SITES

Akhlah: Passover (Pesach)
akhlah.com/jewish-holidays/passover

Kiddle: Passover Facts for Kids
kids.kiddle.co/Passover

PJ Library: What Happens at a Seder?
pjlibrary.org/beyond-books/pjblog/february-2019/what-happens-at-a-seder

INDEX

ABOUT THE AUTHOR

A public and a school librarian, Gloria Koster belongs to the Children's Book Committee of Bank Street College of Education. She enjoys both city and country life, dividing her time between Manhattan and the small town of Pound Ridge, New York. Gloria has three adult children and a bunch of energetic grandkids.